How to Relax

Relax your Mind and Body with 9 Proven Techniques You Can Start Right NOW

Stacy Relax

How To Relax Publishing

Your Free Gift

As a way of saying thanks for your purchase of our book, we made a gift for you containing 2 uncommon relaxation techniques which did not fit into the How To Relax Book and our exclusive **Guided Audio Meditation** which normally sells for 5$, but here you will get it for FREE.

- Bonus 1 helps you to relief stress instantly when used shortly after a stressful event.

- Bonus 2 helps you to prevent stress from creeping up and clearing your mind. It works even on a train during rush hour.

- Bonus 3 An Exclusive Guided Meditation Session to Calm down as an instant Mp3 Download. This normally costs 5$ but here you will get it for free.

Download at http://bit.ly/2fvySqa

How to Relax
Stacy Relax

Published in 2016 by Jens Boje

Pfungststr. 3
60314 Frankfurt
Germany

On the web: *http://how-to-relax.com*
Please send errors to *hello@how-to-relax.com*

Publisher: Jens Boje
Illustration on Cover: Designed by Dooder / Freepik

Copyright © 2016 Jens Boje

Disclaimer

The author and publisher of this book are not responsible in any manner whatsoever for any injury that may occur through following the instructions contained in this book. The activities, physical and otherwise, described herein for informational purposes only, may be too strenuous or dangerous for some people and the reader should consult a physician before doing them.

Your body is your own responsibility; so look after it.

Table of Contents

Introduction

It was a Friday, and we had planned for a family dining at the Italian restaurant that had opened a few blocks away from our home. But I was having a very hectic day at the office. There was a deadline to be met – a presentation to be completed - and a meeting which was unavoidable! I reached home, of course, late into the night. My daughter had waited long and hit the bed after her father coaxed her for a dine out next week.

I felt irritate and frustrated. My neck and back were feeling stiff from the long hours. Being a software developer was no fun. I had to sit in front of the computer for long hours, taking work back home. Stress started creeping up, but by the time I realized, I was neck deep in stress and anxiety.

I couldn't recollect the last time when I slept properly. I was not sleeping; it was more of a tossing around in bed. I missed the time I spent with my daughter. I tried all the standard methods of relaxation – watching television, playing games, browsing through videos, but alas, nothing worked!

I joined a nearby gym with the hope of getting permanent relief, but the results were short-lived. That was when I decided that enough was enough. I made up my mind to find out a permanent solution for my never-ending troubles when I noticed this yoga studio nearby.

It had various types of yoga classes along with meditation and breathing techniques. I chose Yin Yoga along with meditation and breathing. I started experiencing a sense of calmness and serenity like never before, but I still felt I lacked something. This was when I met a person who changed my life forever.

He told me about two fabulous relaxation techniques which worked on the fundamental principle of calming the mind by releasing the physical tension. And, I began my journey with Progressive Muscle Relaxation and Self Myofascial Release. It has been about a year now, and I have started seeing visible differences in my life.

I now have more time for myself and my family. My neck and back hurt less now. I can work without harming myself now!

If you are reading this book at this moment, I am sure that you would be traversing the path that I once had been treading. In this book, I have tried to explain some of the relaxation techniques which I found effective for myself. And, I hope this book benefits everyone!

There is nothing in this world which you cannot change. You just have to commit, practice and be persistent!

Take care!

How to Find a Relaxation Technique Which is Perfect for You?

Stress is omnipresent and hence, it is essential to learn and embrace a relaxation technique. Wait! Relaxation does not mean you are munching popcorn or potato chips while watching television. You have to activate the innate relaxation response of your body to combat and eliminate stress. You can do this by incorporating relaxation techniques such as deep breathing, yoga, Tai Chi, and/or meditation in your life.

Along with reducing your stress, it also improves your energy, mood, health, and overall quality of life. But since each person is different, the effect of each of these techniques will vary with persons. There are certain criteria you should consider before choosing a technique, failing which you are bound to spring back to the initial state.

Always choose a method that resonates with the style of your life. Your response to stress is yet another major point that you should remember while selecting a way of relaxation. There are three primary ways your body reacts to stress.

1. The 'Flight' mode: If you become angry, restless, or disturbed when under stress, you showcase a Flight response. In such cases, techniques such as Yin Yoga, meditation, deep breathing, and progressive muscle relaxation could be right for you as they work towards calming your mind.

2.   The 'Fight' mode: If you withdraw yourself or become silent or depressed under stressful conditions, you showcase a Fight response. Aim for techniques that will stimulate your nervous system, thus helping you manage stress. Pilates, mindfulness, and Power or Ashtanga Yoga would be ideal choices.

3.   The immobilization mode: If you tend to freeze during stressful moments, you deactivate your nervous system. Under such conditions, it becomes essential to mobilize your nervous system to prepare it for either of the responses mentioned above. Tai Chi, Myofascial Release, and Autogenic Training or any other technique that involves mindful movement of the limbs would be right for you.

You can either choose one of these techniques or try a combination of two or more techniques according to the way you respond. Keep in mind your fitness, lifestyle, needs, preferences, and level of stress you encounter daily while choosing the one ideal for you.

So, is it important to pick a technique that is perfect for you? Yes, it is as that will determine how consistently and regularly you will stick on to the program. I had chosen only those technique which I was able to practice, even when amidst a super busy schedule, which is why I succeeded.

Relaxation techniques might give you results with the first stint itself, but you have to commit to practicing regularly to reap the benefits on a long term. The key is to identify a relaxation program that you will adhere to even under busy schedules. While these techniques do help in managing and coping up with stress in a better way, it also improves the overall quality of your life. You should make them integral and inevitable components of your life to experience the changes they gift you.

Now, it is time for us to take a look at some of the most effective relaxation techniques that have changed my life for the good.

Breathing: Purify Your Mind and Body with Air

Everyone takes breathing for granted. It is an innate activity which is essential for life to sustain on this earth. But the same breath comes to your rescue when you are under huge pressure and tension. It doesn't complain about the way you neglect it. It just fills you with an intense sense of relaxation and peace, allowing you to let go of the heaviness mounting in your mind.

Breathing is the foundation for all stress management techniques. It is so simple, yet so versatile that nothing could replace it. If you want to vanquish stress and live in this moment happily, you ought to live with the breath. It is one of the greatest gifts from nature for which you should be truly grateful.

Learning to breathe right will not only ward off anxiety and tension but also improve your overall health and well-being.

Why You Should Learn to Breathe Right?

Breathing right helps you in numerous ways:

- Detoxifies the body by expelling the toxins
- Promotes enhanced circulation of blood
- Calms you and helps you stay focused
- Gifts you better sleep
- Improves your energy levels

Who Should Learn Breathing for Stress Relief?

Each and every person should be aware of this simple stress-busting technique as you can practice it at any time and place. Few rounds of correct breaths are sufficient to boost your energy and shift your focus. It will also help the person to center himself without falling prey to distractions.

One Breathing Technique You Should Try

There are numerous techniques that could help in keeping yourself at ease when you are hit by a storm. While certain breathing techniques take time and patience to master, this particular method is easy to learn.
Deep abdominal breathing is one of the most basic styles of breathing which a person can master very easily. It has various names – belly breathing, diaphragmatic breathing, calm breathing, and so on. At the end of the day, the process is the same.

How to Practice

1. Sit in a comfortable posture where your spine is long and straight. Imagine someone pulling your chest up and high and feel the space between your navel and chest lengthening and expanding.

2. Choose a place where you will remain focused, away from all distractions. Turn off your mobile phone.

3. Place the right palm flat on the abdomen. Your right thumb should rest on your navel.

4. Take a sleep, deep breath, in through your nose for a count of 4, allowing your abdomen to expand and rise. Try to keep your chest in place.

5. Breathe out very slowly and evenly through the mouth for a count of 8, allowing the abdomen to fall inward towards the spine.

6. Keep the exhalations twice as long as the inhalations. Longer exhalations help in calming the body and mind.

7. This completes one round. Practice 10 to 15 rounds.

8. To come out, slowly and naturally resume your natural breathing pace.

Benefits of Deep Abdominal Breathing

1. Less stress and more awareness

2. Massages the internal organs

3. Tones the nervous system

Tips & Caution

1. If you feel lightheaded or dizzy, please discontinue the practice immediately by restoring your natural breathing rhythm.

You just need a couple of minutes to practice this. Try it after a working break or in between a meeting and you will know how beautifully the breath guides you into a state of calmness and relaxation.

Meditation: Learning to Let Go

People have used meditation, since time unknown, to let go of stress and embrace peace and tranquility. It helps you to move beyond the chaos and aid you to ground and focus in the now. Even though there exist countless types of meditation techniques, the aim is singular – learn to become mindfully aware and let go.

One of the most effective meditation techniques is Mantra meditation. Mantra need not necessarily be related to religious concepts. It is just a word or sound that you can repeat to bring back your focus while you meditate.

Learn to let go of the stress triggers, become the observer and live in the present with Mantra meditation!

Why You Should Meditate?

You should meditate for stress relief. But there are more reasons for including meditation in your daily life.

- Improves your overall health and well-being
- Eases physical and mental tension
- Gifts you a better sleep
- Keeps you energetic and focused
- Enhances self-awareness and compassion

Who Should Practice?

Everyone should practice meditation. It does not matter how you respond to stress – flight or fight, meditation helps you do both in a better way. Just spend 15 minutes a day in a calm, serene place and you will soon notice the way your life is changing.

One Meditation Technique You Should Try

As mentioned above, mantra meditation technique is what I would like you to try. It is simple. You can choose any mantra, right from Om to any positive affirmation you love. I use the mantra "Om" to meditate when I am stressed.

Om resonates at 432 Hertz, fetching a sense of universal harmony into our inner being.

How to Practice

1. Sit down in a comfortable seated posture in a place where you will not be disturbed for the next 15 minutes.

2. Keep your spine erect. Close your eyes and let your neck, shoulders, and hands relax.

3. Take a deep breath in and allow each and every cell of your body relax. Exhale and relax further.

4. Take ten rounds of deep inhalations and exhalations to allow your body and mind prepare for the practice.

5. Repeat the mantra "Om" silently or out loudly, depending on your comfort level. Begin each chant with the inhalation and end with the exhalation.

6. Focus on the mantra. If you feel your mind is wandering, bring it back to the present with your affirmation.

7. After a few rounds, you will notice that there exists a synchronicity between your mantra chanting and breath. Make sure that mantra follows the breathing and not vice versa.

8. Let go of any concerns about the way you are chanting the mantra. There is no hard and fast rules of repeating the chant. Choose a way that resonates with your inner self.

9. To end your mantra meditation, slowly reduce the intensity of your chanting. Let the vibration of your chants fill your senses.

10. Remain in silence as you tune into the vibrations.

11. Gently move your toes and fingers. Move your head from side to side. Rub your palms to generate heat. Place the palms on your closed eyes. Gently open your eyes and look into the palms.

12. Join your palms at Heart center and fold forward to extend gratitude to the Universe for replenishing your energy levels.

Tips

1. You can sit on a chair or against a wall. The idea is to keep the spine erect to ensure unobstructed flow of energy throughout the practice. Feel free to sit on folded blankets or bolster for keeping the spine straight.

Meditation brings in spontaneous results, but as you make it an integral element of your daily life, your life will change miraculously!

Yin Yoga: Find Your Serenity

Yin yoga is a slow-paced mind-body practice where you hold the postures or Asanas for longer duration, say two to twenty minutes, with the focus on conscious breathing and relaxation. It is more of a meditative style of practice where you do not sweat and almost anyone can do it.

Yin yoga can help lower stress, let go of anxiety, and improve your flexibility. It gives you an opportunity to enjoy peacefulness without forcing your body into poses. A restorative form of practice, it allows you to use props and encourages the practitioners to listen to the cues your body gives.

The focus is on spine, hips, pelvis, inner thighs, and groin, where your body tends to store stress and anxiety more. The challenge here is to hold the poses for the entirety of the time without moving.

Why You Should Do Yin Yoga?

Yin yoga offers some exciting benefits which tempts you to indulge in it:

- Eases stress and anxiety and clears your mind

- Teaches you to live in the moment

- Helps you let go of anything and everything that does not serve you at the moment

- Improves circulation and flexibility

- Stimulates the flow of energy through the meridians

Who Should Practice Yin Yoga?

Anyone who would love to say goodbye to stress and anxiety from their life can practice this style of yoga. If you love a serene and tranquil approach to stress management, then this technique is yours for sure. Every practice takes you through an entirely enticing journey, allowing you to release, surrender, and let go.

If you tend to withdraw yourself into a cocoon and curl up in your sanctuary, then practice Yin Yoga to bring in some energy, love, and peace into your life.

One Yin Yoga Pose You Could Try

A classical Yin Yoga session could last anywhere between 30 to 90 minutes. However, if you do not have the time with you and you want to relax instantly, then this pose is the right one.

Anahatasana, or the Melting Heart, is what I am talking about. I just love this. Scoop your body like a small baby and just breathe.

How to Practice

1. Come down on all your fours. Adjust your body to stack the wrists under shoulders and knees under hips.

2. Curl the toes and walk the fingertips a few inches in front of you, allowing the chest to rest on the mat. Make sure that the hands are shoulder-width apart.

3. Inhale slowly and deeply into your stomach.

4. As you exhale, push your buttocks towards the heels, but only till halfway so that your tailbone faces the ceiling. Keep the elbows off the floor/mat.

5. Place your forehead on the space in between your active arms. Relax the neck and shoulders. Press through the palms and push your hips to the ceiling at the same time to lengthen your spine.

6. Hold the pose for 5 minutes, breathing deeply into it, allowing each and every muscle to relax.

7. To come out of the pose, gently slide your body completely on the floor, stretching out your legs.

Benefits of Anahatasana

1. Stretches your shoulders, neck, and spine

2. Stimulates your abdominal organs

3. Detoxifies liver and spleen

Tips & Cautions

1. Place a folded blanket or use a bolster if your fore-head is not touching the floor naturally. Do not force your body into the pose like other yoga classes.

2. Add additional cushioning for your knees if you have acute or chronic knee or ligament injuries. You can do it anywhere and at anytime you want to de-stress and unwind. So, try it now and feel the difference.

Mindfulness: Releasing the Past

How many people live in the present? Many are stuck either in the past or worried about the future. Does this sound familiar to you? The failure to appreciate and live in the present could be one of the primary reasons for stress. Mindfulness is an art which teaches you to be consciously aware of yourself, your emotions, thoughts, and feelings that prevail in the present moment.

Mindfulness, which is a meditation technique adapted from the Vipassana Mediation, helps you break free of your past and future. It helps to ground and center and feel the bliss of this moment. It teaches you to become an observer without any judgments.

Practicing this stress relief technique helps you to intentionally become aware of your thoughts. To put it simple words, being mindful will help you to realize a golden truth – "Past is past, future is unknown; it is only the present that we know."

According to studies, the practice of mindfulness shares an inverse relationship with depression and stress. Being mindful helps in reducing worries and rumination, inculcation a sense of peace and calmness.

Why You Should Practice?

- Here are some cool reasons for being mindful!
- Lesser stress, anxiety, and tension
- Improved body-mind-soul connection

- Feel happier and more joyful
- Improved self-compassion and love for others
- Better focus and memory

Who Should Practice?

Every person who wants to be happy, calm, and relaxed should practice mindfulness. It just allows you to experience the serenity you would love to stay with forever. 10 minutes of mindfulness a day is the key to a happier, stress-free life.

How to Practice?

There are various ways of practicing mindfulness, but ultimately the goal is the same – to help you stay alerted and relax by intentionally watching your mind hopping around without any judgment. You can practice this stress-busting technique anytime and anywhere, but until you master it, please make sure that you are dedicatedly practicing in a place where you are alone.

1. Sit down in a comfortable seated posture or lie down on your back. Choose a place that is silent and serene and where you will remain undisturbed for the next few minutes.

2. If you are sitting, make sure that your spine is erect and aligned with your spine. Keep your head, neck, and shoulders relaxed. Sit in a comfortable way without stooping or hunching or being rigid.

3. Close your eyes to prevent distractions.

4. Become aware of the way you are sitting. Feel the sensations. Just observe. Do not try to forcibly sit in a particular way. Just maintain your natural state.

5. Now, become aware of your breathing. Feel the air flowing in through your nostrils and filling each and every cell of your body. Breathe naturally. Do not try to modify your breath. Just be aware of the way air flows into and out of your body.

6. Slowly, move your focus to your thoughts. Allow the thoughts to flow naturally. Let your mind hop from one thought to the next. Observe and feel the way thoughts appear and disappear. Do not judge.

7. If your mind starts wandering, bring it back gently to the present moment in a natural way, allowing your thoughts to follow their natural trail.

8. Once you are ready to come out, take a couple of deep breaths and return to the present.
   You can practice initially for 15 minutes. Once you master, increase your mindfulness meditation to 30 minutes, twice a day.

Mastering mindfulness is tricky; but once you are there, you will enjoy a stress-free life. Try it and feel the difference!

Qi Gong: Unclog Your Blocked Energy Channels

According to Chinese traditions, an obstruction in the path of Qi [pronounced as chee] triggers undesirable health conditions, including aches and pains. Qi Gong was designed as body and mind wellness practice to unclog these energy channels so that Qi flows unimpeded, paving way for a healthier you.

Despite its ancient origin, the modern day studies suggest the effectiveness of qigong exercise in reducing stress and anxiety. The movements are very slow with focus on breath, which gives you the potential to offset the adverse impacts of modern lifestyle's tension and anxiety. It is more of a preventive measure.

In simple words, Qi Gong is not just a healing solution, but it is a form of well-being.

Why You Should Practice Qi Gong?

Some of the benefits you can reap by incorporating Qi Gong in your lifestyle include:

* Improved health and well-being

* Clear and tranquil mind

* Deeper, restorative sleep

* Improved energy levels

* Enhanced happiness and concentration

Who Should Practice?

If you have the tendency to become angry or agitated under strain, Qi Gong could be your stress management technique. It will help in keeping you healthy by reducing your tension. A short routine is sufficient to unblock the channels and set the energy flowing, making your relaxed and energized.

One Qi Gong Technique You Could Try

This technique does not involve any physical movement. Rather, it teaches you to relax by breathing. You can do it anywhere and at anytime, but make sure that you are not interrupted or distracted during your practice.

Wave breathing, as it is known, is a technique that brings in instant stress relief. I love this technique and use it quite often before I attend my meetings to calm myself.

How to Practice

1. Sit down on a chair, keeping your spine upright. Let the tip of your tongue touch lazily on the upper palette.
2. Relax your neck and shoulders consciously. Close your eyes naturally and just allow yourself to indulge in this sense of calmness and peace as air flows into and out of your body in an effortless way.

3. Place your right palm on your lower abdomen and left palm on your chest.

4. Take a slow, deep inhalation, breathing first into your lower abdomen, then into your rib cage, and finally into your chest, allowing each of the parts to inflate naturally while the shoulder lifts up.

5. As you exhale slowly, allow your shoulders to sink, emptying the air from the chest followed the rib cage, and then the abdomen, pulling the stomach close to the spine.

6. With each inhalation, allow peace, tranquility, and relaxation to fill each and every cell of your body. With each exhalation, release stress, tension, and anxiety to flow out of your body, mind, and soul.

7. Practice for 5 minutes to experience how the body and mind expand as the lightness fills in you with exhalations.

8. Once you are completely relaxed, restore your natural breathing pattern.

9. Rub your palms to generate heat. Place it over your closed eyes. Gently open your eyes and look into your palms.

Benefits of Wave Breathing

1. Unwinds and relaxes your body and mind
2. Gives you a sense of lightness
3. Inculcates a sense of peace and tranquility

As I said, just a couple of minutes would gift you with relaxation, and when you delve deeper, you will notice the optimistic and blissful disposition Qi Gong gifts you!

Progressive Muscle Relaxation: Relax Your Muscles for a Calmer Mind

Progressive muscle relaxation, as the name implies, works towards creating mental tranquility by relaxing physically. Edmund Jacobson was the first to talk about this stress management technique, way back in the 1930s.

In simple words, it is a dual step process which works by tensing and relaxing a particular group of muscles in a systematic way. The technique helps you become aware of the way your muscles and entire body reacts when stressed and relaxed.

And, this awareness makes your mind calm when you are stressed and worried.

Why You Should Practice Progressive Muscle Relaxation?

This technique helps in alleviating stress and anxiety, but it offers some other benefits as well.

* Relieves insomnia

* Eases inflammation and helps with chronic pain management

* Manages hypertension

* Helpful in managing post-traumatic stress disorder

* Improves memory

Who Should Practice?

If you tend to become immobilized, physically and mentally, when under stress or trauma, then this systematic relaxation method is meant for you. It arouses your nervous system and prepares it for combating stress.

The Technique

There are two ways of practicing this technique. While one method works from toes to head, the second one works vice versa – head to toes. Either way, the muscle groups are tensed for 5 to 10 seconds before allowing them to go limp for about 20 seconds.

The method mentioned below works in the following order.

- Foot
- Calf
- Thighs
- Hips
- Buttocks
- Stomach
- Chest
- Back
- Arms and hands
- Neck and shoulders
- Face

You tense and release the muscle groups on your right first after which the focus shifts to your left side. Make sure you complete one group of muscles before moving to the next.

You can practice this stress management technique either by sitting or lying down. Breathing is the key here; so remember to breathe through the entire process to reap the benefits.

How to Practice

1. Choose a comfortable position in a place where you will not be interrupted for the next 15 to 20 minutes. If you are sitting, make sure that your spine is straight, yet relaxed.

2. Close your eyes and focus on your body. Allow your mind to focus of each of the muscles.

3. Take a slow, deep breath into your stomach. Retain the breath for a count of 4, and exhale completely.

4. Again, take a deep breath for a count of 4, allowing your abdomen to rise first followed by the lungs.

5. As you expel the air out, allow your lungs fall in first followed by the stomach. While exhaling, imagine the tension flowing out of your body.

6. Keep inhaling and exhaling till you feel your body beginning to relax. Once you body starts relaxing, move to the next step.

7. Focus on your right foot and become aware of how it feels. Slowly squeeze and tense the muscles of

your right foot and hold it for a count of ten. Take slow, deep breaths.

8. Allow the muscles to go limp by relaxing the foot and releasing the tension. Stay here for a count of twenty, breathing deeply and slowly.

9. Once you complete with the right side, repeat the same tense and release sequence with your left foot.

10. Slowly, move up towards your face, tensing and relaxing each of the muscle groups as mentioned above, allowing the tension to release completely as you reach the face.

11. Once you complete the entire sequence, relax with your eyes closed for a couple of normal breaths to allow your body to return to its natural state.

Tips

1. Practice the technique daily for 15 to 30 days until you master it. Once you master, you will be able to do it at the drop of a hat.

2. There is a shorter version of this practice which you can try when you have less time. It's grouped into the lower limb, chest and abdomen, arms, neck, shoulders, and face.

3. Avoid the muscle group(s) if they are under strain or pain.

Make sure you consult a doctor before practicing this stress release mechanism if you have hypertension or history of back injury.

Pilates: Move Your Core to Eliminate Stress

Does Pilates help reduce stress? Is it not a core-strengthening and abs developing workout session? I also felt the same when my friend suggested me to try Pilates for stress management. And, the results were mind-blowing.

Pilates helps reduce stress. The focus is on breathing right, and when you become aware of your body through your breath, your stress will melt away. From the view of science, Pilates workouts lower the stress hormones, simultaneously triggering the release of feel good hormones – dopamine, serotonin, and all other endorphins, calming you physically, emotionally, and soulfully.

Stress targets your abdominal muscles more and so does Pilates. This is why people choose this workout form to tone their core. But very few are aware of the fact that they are undoing the damages induced by stress. As tension eases, your core starts shaping up.

Why Should You do Pilates?

Some of the tempting benefits [other than stress management] that Pilates offers include:

* Improved flexibility, muscular strength, and physical coordination

* Lean, healthier body, and mind

- Stronger and more flexible spine
- Better focus and concentration
- Better awareness

Who Should Practice?

Anyone can practice this form of exercise. It is just fun. If you love to sweat out your stress, then this workout regimen is for you. If you give yourself an honest effort, I am sure you will love this stress-busting exercise.

Include 2 to 3 sessions of Pilates per week in your training regimen to notice positive changes.

One Pilates Move You Could Try

Ideally, a pilates workout session could last anywhere between 30 to 90 minutes, depending on the intention of the class. But if you are searching for that instant stress busting solution, then this one would be the right choice.

The Rolling like a ball is one of my favorite of all Pilates stretching series. It stretches and massages your entire body in such a playful, yet elegant way and is great for eliminating bloating and upset stomachs. Not only does it feel fantastic, but it will relieve the tension from your body and mind.

How to Practice

1. Sit down on an exercise mat or floor.

2. Bend your knees, separating them as wide as your shoulders, and hug your thighs into your chest. Clasp your hands around your ankles. Flex your toes away from your body.

3. Make sure that your sitting bones are resting on the mat. Tuck your chin slightly towards your chest.

4. Engage your core, pulling the abdominal muscles towards your spine.

5. Inhale and roll back, rounding your shoulder blades down and away from the ears.

6. Exhale and come back to starting position.

7. Keep rolling for 5 minutes, breathing deeply, allowing your body and mind to relax.

8. To exit, extend your legs and shake them out.

Try to maintain the natural curve of your spine, while pulling the navel close to the spine as you roll. Do not hurry. Ensure that you are rolling back and forth, vertebra by vertebra to avoid sudden jerks and back injuries.

Benefits of Rolling Like A Ball

1. Massages and stretches the entire body

2. Improves flexibility

3. Massages your abdomen and expels trapped gas

For faster results, increase the duration of rolling per week.

Tips & Cautions

1. If you have knee, ligament, or back injuries, please be careful while performing the exercise.

2. Keep your neck relaxed while rolling back and forth.

3. If you are not able to hold the ankles from outside, clasp your hands under the shins.
    A typical Pilates sessions would include a pre-designed set of exercises and stretches. Try it and feel the difference!

Autogenic Training: Relax Yourself Using Your Thoughts

This stress busting technique works on a simple universal principle of life – "You are what your thoughts create". Whatever you see in the physical realm would have already happened in your mind. It is just the reflection that you see. Using this principle, AT, as it is known popularly teaches you to relax your body and mind and reduce stress.

It was developed by Johannes Heinrich Schultz, a German neurologist during the 1920s. It aims to help people relax at their will, without worrying about the place and time.

You cannot expect to see immediate results, but those who master can combat chronic stress effectively. And, it takes about six months to master this stress management method.

Why You Should Practice Autogenic Training?

In general, people use this technique to manage and combat stress. However, it offers some other benefits as well.

- Helps in managing fatigue, anxiety, and irritability

- Helps in pain management

- Helps in easing insomnia

- Could help in managing conditions such as constipation and hypertension

- Enhances self-empowerment and self-control

Who Should Practice?

Autogenic training is quite similar to self-hypnosis. It is ideal for those who tend to become agitated or angry when under stress. This method helps in making them more mindful and manage the situations with control.

The Autogenic Training Technique

You just need 10 minutes to say goodbye to stress, once you master the practice. It comprises six exercises whose goal is to make your body heavy, warm, and relaxed. Just sit down in a comfortable, reclining posture and listen to the commands without setting any intention. Visualize the verbal cues and use it to relax your body and mind.

The six exercises include:

- Inducing a sense of heaviness
- Inducing warmth
- Calming your heartbeat
- Breathing
- Abdomen
- Cool forehead

How to Practice

1. Lie down in a comfortable posture in a place where you will remain undisturbed and undistracted during the practice.

2. Let your legs fall to the sides naturally. Relax your arms, slightly away from the armpits, at your sides.

3. Take six rounds of slow and deep breaths to allow yourself to set into the process.

4. Once you are ready, say the statements mentioned below to yourself in a slow, yet convincing way. Repeat each statement 6 to 8 times before moving to the next.

5. Try to visualize the sensation you experience as you repeat the statements to relax deeper.

6. After you complete the practice, take a few rounds of deep breaths. Open your eyes slowly and lie down for a few seconds before moving.
    A typical Autogenic Training script would be something as given below.

7. My arms are getting heavy. My left arm is getting heavy. My right arm is getting heavy. Both of my arms are getting heavy.

8. My legs are getting heavy. My left leg is getting heavy. My right arm is getting heavy. Both of my arms are getting heavy.

9. My arms are becoming warm. My left arm is becoming warm. My right arm is becoming warm. Both of my arms are becoming warm.

10. My legs are becoming warm. My left leg is becoming warm. My right arm is becoming warm. Both of my arms are becoming warm.

11. My heartbeat is becoming steady and calm.

12. My breathing is becoming steady and calm.

13. My abdomen is becoming warm and soft.

14. My forehead is becoming cool.

Tips

Therapists recommend practicing autogenic exercise 3 times per day to see results.

You can either use your own voice or choose a recording.

If you are using AT as a solution for any medical condition, please talk to your physician so that you can use it as a complementary therapy.

While autogenic training is quite an effective solution for stress, one needs to practice it regularly and dedicatedly to reap in the true results.

Self Myofascial Release: Release Your Physical Tension to Ward Off Stress

Self Myofascial release cannot be counted as a classic stress management technique. It actually works on the basic principle of body-mind connection, just like other stress relief methods. According to the pioneers of myofascial release, your tissue also has a memory which stores all unpleasant events, which in turn manifest in the form of health conditions such as inflammation and pain.

SMR, as it is known, is a technique that stretches your tissues, releases the tension stored in your fascia, and restore the natural posture and alignment. Fascia is what supports and strengthens your body. But, unfortunately, it constricts due to various triggers, with chronic stress being a prominent one, leading to tight muscles. This body work aims to release this constriction, thus easing the symptoms of chronic stress, physically and emotionally.

There are various tools you can use to practice SMR – foam rollers, handheld rollers, and medicinal balls, to name a few. Irrespective of the tool used, this technique, aims to do away with the adhesions and restore the natural functioning of the affected muscles. When your body is at peace, your mind will, naturally, calm down.

Why You Should Try Self Myofascial Release?

Along with offering your freedom from physical and mental tension, SMR is also beneficial in the following way:

- Restores the natural balances of your muscles and improves joint motion

- Eases soreness and stress experienced by muscles

- Enhances neuromuscular efficiency

- Eases muscular constriction

- Reduces adverse impacts of stress on your body

Who Should Practice?

If you are a chronic worrier and find it unable to respond to the stress trigger and suffering from intense, painful, inflammatory health conditions, do practice this. But, make sure that you consult your physician and follow his advice before experimenting with SMR.

The Myofascial Release Technique

According to the advocates of SMR, the trauma of your past experiences tends to get stored in the connective tissues of your body, triggering stress and preventing smooth circulation, which in turn leads to diseases. SMR is known to be effective in helping your tissues let go that trauma, setting you free.

The technique outlined here uses the foam roller, which helps you to practice this technique at home. It is ideal to learn the technique from a certified therapist before you practice at home to see long term benefits.

How to Practice

1. Roll yourself on a foam roller until you feel the trigger point or the point where are hurt.

2. Stop at that point and rest on your roller for 30 to 60 seconds. If you feel any kind of pain, stop rolling, and rest the painful zone for 45 seconds.

3. Pull your navel to the spine while rolling to keeping your lumbar-pelvic-hip complex stable during the technique.

4. Once you practice, wait for the next 24 to 48 hours for the muscle soreness to subside before further practice.

Here Is a Sample SMR Technique For Your Upper Back:

1. Place a foam roller at the base of your rib cage.

2. Lean back on the roller, keeping knees perpendicular to the floor.

3. lowly roll up and down, pausing on any spot you feel the pain, in a gentle way.

4. Keeping rolling till your roller reaches the two large triangular muscles on your back just below your shoulders. Arch your back and place the crown of the head on the floor and hold this posture.

5. Inhale and lift your arms up. Exhale and hug yourself.

6. Repeat the lifts and hugs 15 times.

7. Once ready, slowly roll back the roller down to the spine.

8. Gently roll on to your sides and sit up.

9. Relax for a few seconds before moving on to the next set of exercises.

Tips & Caution

1. Always choose a foam roller that is neither too hard nor too soft.

2. Avoid rolling if you experience pain at any given point. Continuing to roll on painful spots increases tightness and worsens your pain.

3. Since the areas of the spine located in the lower back and neck are unprotected, those regions are vulnerable to injuries. So it is advisable to roll only on the upper back as the back muscles and shoulder blades shield the spine.

While this efficient and straightforward technique delivers active, feel good results, it is advisable to learn the technique thoroughly before practicing at home.

What You Should Do Next

I believe there is not just one technique working for all of us. Each of us has individual needs and wants. Most of the time you do not know in advance if a method fits you. It is a journey; one you need to go and experience many of the methods yourself.

Try the exercises in the book and whichever resonates best with you, start to dig deeper into that particular relaxation technique. From there you can explore the others.

You will find additional resources on the How to Relax! Resource Page (http://how-to-relax.com/resources/) to get more inspiration and tips for your journey.

Thank You

You have just one life. To live it to its fullest extent, you ought to be relaxed, calm, and live in the present. All the relaxation methods in the book help you with this task. Trust the mechanisms. Love and forgive yourself and you will find that life is a beautiful gift!

When it helps you, please give me a hand in helping more people and leave an honest review.

Take care and stay safe!

Discover More Books by How to Relax

Meditation for Beginners

http://bit.ly/2fPvfPD

5 Simple and Effective Techniques To Calm your Mind, Gain Focus, Inner Peace and Happiness

Minimalism Sucks

http://bit.ly/2fzd1AD

The lifestyle of de-cluttering and living better with less can also help you to find relaxation.

Printed in Great Britain
by Amazon